AF605481

BACKYARD
Tennis

This book is dedicated to all the deadly remote outback kids hanging with mates, learning new things and chasing dreams. And to readers all over Australia with open eyes, minds and hearts. And to my children Deklan and Ailee, my nieces, nephews and grandkids.

A special thank you to the black&write! fellowship team, Hachette team, Alex Adsett (agent), Shel Sweeney (writing mentor and editor from A Worded Life), and Hakea Hustler.

And a huge thank you to talented illustrator Samantha Campbell for her work on this series, and many of my other books.

– C.M.

For my daughter Nevayah.

– S.C.

Carl Merrison illustrated by Samantha Campbell

Mum loves tennis, but we don't have a court out here.

One day, she gets out her old racquets and takes me into the backyard.

'I'll teach you how to play,' Mum says.

Chelsea pops her head over our fence.

'What you mob doing?' she asks.

'Come and play!' we say.

Chelsea joins my team.

We play doubles.

Tkai pops his head over our fence.

'What you mob doing?' he asks.

'Come and play!' we say.

Mum is the umpire.
I am the crowd.

Chelsea and Tkai play their match.

Jah'lae pops her head over our fence.

'What you mob doing?' she asks.

'Come and play!' we say.

We take turns playing our matches.

I am the umpire.

Mum is the food van.

Chelsea is the crowd.

Tkai and Jah'lae play their match.

Angel pops her head over the side gate.

'What you mob doing?' she asks.

'Come and play!' we say.

WELCOME

It's too crowded in our backyard stadium,

so we move to a **bigger** one for our main event.

Mum has a deadly serve but my forehand is strong.

We rally and the crowd goes wild.

Turns out I **LOVE** tennis too.

This manuscript won State Library of Queensland's black&write! Fellowship.

A Lothian Children's Book
First published in Australia and New Zealand in 2024
by Hachette Australia
Gadigal Country, Level 17, 207 Kent Street, Sydney NSW 2000
www.hachettechildrens.com.au

This edition published in 2026.

Hachette Australia acknowledges and pays our respects to the past and present Traditional Owners and Custodians of Country throughout Australia and recognises the continuation of cultural, spiritual and educational practices of Aboriginal and Torres Strait Islander peoples. Our head office is located on the lands of the Gadigal people of the Eora Nation.

Author photograph courtesy Amber Melody Portrait Studio
Illustrator photograph courtesy Gabrielle Fry

A catalogue record for this work is available from the National Library of Australia

The authorised representative in the EEA is Hachette Ireland,
8 Castlecourt Centre, Dublin 15, D15 XTP3, Ireland (email: info@hbgi.ie)

ISBN: 978 0 7344 2423 5 (paperback)

Designed by Liz Seymour
Printed in China by 1010 Printing International Limited